AF251077

The Unofficial Schitt's Creek Cookbook

365-Days Amazing & Delicious Recipes for Schitt's Creek Fans

Jeanette Slater

© Copyright 2021 - All rights reserved.

Table of Contents

Introduction

Hey, Schitt's Creek Fans! Do you want to take a trip to Elmdale County and enjoy the best of its delights from your very favourite hamlet- Schitt Creek? Well, The Unofficial Schitt's Creek Cookbook is here to give you all the delicious meal inspired by this popular show. Whether you are an expert at cooking or does not know a dime about cooking, these simple and quick recipes will help you prepare some amazing Schitt's Creek style meal in no time. From Café Tropical's dishes to Jocelyn's flavoursome meals and delights from the famous Rosebud Motel, you can find all the inspired recipes in this cookbook. Each recipe is created using basic and easy to get ingredients so that you could try them any day.

This cookbook has many recipes and features drinks, appetizers, entrees, desserts, and entrees so that you can find your favorite meal for any time of the day. Cook these delicious meals and revisit the amazing episodes of your favorite television series. It is a perfect gift to surprise any big Schitt's Creek fan! So, whether you have a friend or a family member, who is crazy about this series, give them this ultimate treat and let your loved ones enjoy some of the best meals from this show, including:

- Sloppy Jocelyn's
- There's a Dead Guy in Room 4-Cheese Macaroni
- Twyla's Meadow Harvest Smoothie
- Farm Witches' Peanut Butter Things
- Rosebud Motel Cinnamon Rolls
- Budd's Bourbon BBQ Sauce

The Unofficial Schitt's Creek Cookbook offers a variety of recipes for people with varying cooking skill. It has easy-to-follow instructions for each recipe which make it possible to cook, ready and enjoy your food right away. So, put on your aprons! And let's do some Schitt creek style cooking!

Enchiladas

Prep Time: 10 minutes.

Cook Time: 40 minutes.

Serves: 6

Ingredients:

Salsa Roja Ingredients:

- 2 cherry red guajillo chilis
- 2 dried ancho chilis
- 2 pasilla chilis
- 2 medium onions, peeled and chopped
- 2 plum tomatoes, halved
- 3 garlic cloves, peeled

Assembly

- 3 cooked chicken breasts, shredded
- 3 poblano peppers, halved and fire-roasted
- 3 tbsp butter

- Water
- 1 pinch Mexican oregano
- 3 large chicken breasts
- Salt, to taste
- Black pepper, to taste

- 3 tbsp flour
- 2 cups whole milk
- 8 oz queso de papa cheddar, shredded

- Additional queso de papa, for topping
- Corn tortillas
- Vegetable oil (for frying tortillas)
- Oaxaca Cheese

Preparation:

1. Roast all the peppers in a dry pan over medium heat for 2 minutes.
2. Transfer to a plate and roast tomatoes, garlic and onions in the pan, then sauté until soft.
3. Stir in peppers, and Mexican oregano, then cook the mixture to a simmer.
4. Add chicken breasts, cover and cook for 15 minutes in the oven.
5. Blend chiles and vegetables in a blender until smooth.
6. Stir in tomato sauce, salt, and black pepper, then blend more.
7. Shred the cooked chicken and keep them aside.
8. Cut the poblano peppers in half and roast them in a pan until roasted.
9. Blend 3 tbsp flour with butter for queso, then transfer to a pan.
10. Cook the flour blend for 2 minutes on low heat.
11. Stir in 2 cup milk and whisk well until smooth and lump-free.
12. Remove from the heat, then add 8 oz. shredded queso de papa.
13. Mix well until smooth.
14. Warm the corn tortillas in a saucepan.
15. Spread the peppers mixture in a shallow dish.
16. Place the tortilla in the pepper mixture.
17. Top the tortilla with shredded chicken, poblano peppers and Oaxaca cheese.
18. Roll the stuffed tortilla and place it in the dish with the seam side down.
19. Repeat the same steps with the remaining filling and tortillas.
20. Add remaining shredded queso dep papa and cheese sauce on top.
21. Bake the enchiladas for 15 minutes in the oven at 400 degrees F.
22. Serve warm.

Serving Suggestion: Serve these lightsabers with whipped cream.

Variation Tip: You can also use blackberries, blueberries, and strawberries to make these lightsabers.

Nutritional Information Per Serving:

Calories 589 | Fat 16g |Sodium 362mg | Carbs 34g | Fiber 0.4g | Sugar 14g | Protein 30g

Amish Pickled Eggs and Beets

Prep Time: 5 minutes.
Cook Time: 5 minutes.
Serves: 6
Ingredients:

- 1 cup cider vinegar
- 1 cup beet juice
- 1/2 cup brown sugar

- 1 teaspoon salt
- 6 hard-boiled eggs, shelled
- 1 (15 oz.) can small round beets

Preparation:

1. Boil beet juice, brown sugar, salt, and vinegar in a saucepan for 5 minutes.
2. Allow the liquid to cool, then add beets and boiled eggs.
3. Cover and refrigerate the eggs overnight.
4. Serve.

Serving Suggestion: Enjoy the eggs with crispy bacon on the side.

Variation Tip: Don't add sugar to restrict the carbs intake.

Nutritional Information Per Serving:
Calories 310 | Fat 5g |Sodium 32mg | Carbs 23g | Fiber 0.4g | Sugar 4g | Protein 32g

Chocolate Pudding

Prep Time: 5 minutes.

Cook Time: 5 minutes.

Serves: 6

Ingredients:

- 2/3 cup sugar
- 1/4 cup Hershey's cocoa
- 3 tablespoons cornstarch
- 1/4 teaspoon salt
- 2-1/4 cups milk
- 2 tablespoons butter
- 1 teaspoon vanilla extract
- Whipped topping

Preparation:

1. Mix sugar, cornstarch, cocoa, salt and milk in a saucepan until lump-free.
2. Cook this mixture over medium heat, then boil for 1 minute.
3. Stir in vanilla and butter, then cook until the mixture thickens.
4. Divide the pudding in the serving bowls and allow them to cool.
5. Refrigerate the pudding for 4 hours.
6. Serve with desired toppings on top.

Serving Suggestion: Serve the pudding with whipped cream on top.

Variation Tip: Add coconut or almond milk instead of milk to make it vegan.

Nutritional Information Per Serving:

Calories 205 | Fat 21g |Sodium 342mg | Carbs 38 | Fiber 0.4g | Sugar 12g | Protein 2.1g

Quiche

Prep Time: 5 minutes.
Cook Time: 45 minutes.
Serves: 8
Ingredients:

- 8 large eggs
- 3/4 cup heavy whipping cream
- 3/4 cup milk
- ½ teaspoon salt
- ½ teaspoon black pepper
- 6 oz. Colby cheese, shredded
- 1 cup cooked ham, diced
- 1/2 cup green onions, chopped
- 1/2 cup mini bell peppers, sliced

Preparation:

1. At 350 degrees F, preheat your oven.
2. Beat eggs, milk, cream, black pepper and salt in a large bowl.
3. Add green onions, ham and Colby, then pour the mixture into a greased 9-inch pie plate.
4. Top the mixture bell peppers, then bake for 45 minutes in the oven.
5. Slice and serve warm.

Serving Suggestion: Serve the quiche with crispy bacon and bread.

Variation Tip: Add colorful bell peppers for a good presentation.

Nutritional Information Per Serving:

Calories 490 | Fat 18g |Sodium 150mg | Carbs 16g | Fiber 0.4g | Sugar 4g | Protein 32g

Bagels

Prep Time: 5 minutes.
Cook Time: 25 minutes.
Serves: 6

Ingredients:

- 1 1/2 cups warm water
- 2 3/4 teaspoons instant dry yeast
- 4 cups bread flour
- 1 tablespoon granulated sugar
- 2 teaspoons salt
- 2 teaspoons olive oil

Egg wash:

- 1 egg white beaten
- 1 tablespoon water

For Boiling

2 quarts water

1/4 cup honey

Preparation:

1. Mix 1 ½ cups warm water and yeast in a bowl, then leave it for 5 minutes.
2. Stir in brown sugar, salt and flour, then mix on low speed for 2 minutes.
3. Transfer the dough onto a floured surface, then knead for 5 minutes.
4. Place the dough in a greased bowl and cover it with aluminium foil.
5. Leave the dough for 2 hours in the kitchen.
6. Layer 2 large baking sheet with parchment paper.
7. Divide the prepared dough into 8 equal pieces and roll each ball into 2 inches in diameter.
8. Place the bagels in a pan, covered until water is ready.
9. At 425 degrees F, preheat your oven.
10. Add 2 quarts of water to a cooking pot and stir in honey.
11. Cook the water to a boil, then add bagels. Cook for 1 minute per side.
12. Transfer the bagels to a plate with a slotted spoon to the baking sheets.
13. Brush the bagels with egg wash and bake for 25 minutes. Rotate the pan once cooked halfway through.
14. Allow the bagels to cool.
15. Serve.

Serving Suggestion: Dip the bagels in maple syrup or chocolate syrup before serving for change of taste.

Variation Tip: Add chopped raisins to the dough.

Nutritional Information Per Serving:

Calories 242 | Fat 12g |Sodium 165mg | Carbs 29g | Fiber 1.4g | Sugar 12g | Protein 11g

Buttermilk Pancakes

Prep Time: 5 minutes.

Cook Time: 10 minutes.

Serves: 6

Ingredients:

- 2 cups all-purpose flour

- 2 ½ cups buttermilk
- 3 tablespoons sugar
- 1 ½ teaspoons baking powder
- 1 ½ teaspoons baking soda
- 1 ¼ teaspoons salt
- 2 eggs
- 3 tablespoons butter, melted
- Vegetable oil for cooking

Preparation:

1. At 325 degrees F, preheat your oven.
2. Mix salt, baking soda, baking powder, sugar and flour in a bowl.
3. Make a well at the centre and pour in buttermilk.
4. Mix well until smooth, then add eggs. And melted butter.
5. Whisk well until lump-free and smooth
6. Set a suitable skillet over low heat for 5 minutes.
7. Pour 1 tbsp oil into the skillet and let it heat.
8. Add 1/3 cup batter into the skillet and spread it evenly.
9. Cook the pancake for 1-2 minutes per side.
10. Transfer the pancakes to a plate and cook more pancakes.
11. Serve.

Serving Suggestion: Enjoy the pancakes with maple syrup on top.

Variation Tip: Add blueberry preserves to the batter.

Nutritional Information Per Serving:
Calories 156 | Fat 7g |Sodium 56mg | Carbs 22.1g | Fiber 2g | Sugar 9g | Protein 14g

Rosé Sangria

Prep Time: 5 minutes.

Cook Time: 0 minutes.

Serves: 2

Ingredients:

- 2 tablespoons lemon juice
- 2 tablespoons brandy
- 1/4 cup sugar
- 1/4 cup orange liqueur
- 1 bottle rose wine
- 2 navel oranges, sliced
- 1-pint raspberries
- 1 cup of sparkling water

Preparation:

1. Mix orange liqueur, sugar, brandy, and lemon juice in a large pitcher.
2. Add raspberries, orange slices and wine.
3. Cover and refrigerate the punch.
4. Serve with sparkling water on the top.

Serving Suggestion: Serve the drink with fresh mint on top.

Variation Tip: Add strawberries instead of raspberries.

Nutritional Information Per Serving:

Calories 148 | Fat 0g |Sodium 200mg | Carbs 26.5g | Fiber 0.9g | Sugar 2g | Protein 3.8g

Mall Pretzel

Prep Time: 5 minutes.

Cook Time: 16 minutes.

Serves: 6

Ingredients:

Dough:

- 1/2 cup whole milk
- 1/2 cup water
- 2 teaspoons yeast
- 2 cups 2 tbsp of all-purpose flour
- 1/3 cup brown sugar
- 1 tsp salt
- 1/2 teaspoon baking powder
- 2 tbsp butter melted

Cooking Solution:

- 2 cups warm water
- 2 tbsp baking soda

Butter Topping:

- 6 tbsp butter melted
- coarse salt

Preparation:

1. Mix ½ cup water and milk in a bowl and heat it for 45 seconds in the microwave oven.
2. Add yeast, mix and leave the mixture for 5 minutes.
3. Stir in salt, baking powder, melted butter, sugar, and flour, then mix in the stand mixer.
4. Knead the prepared dough for 7 minutes at medium-high speed.
5. Grease a bowl, add the dough, cover and leave the dough for 30 minutes.
6. Mix baking with water in a small bowl.
7. At 410 degrees F, preheat your oven.
8. Divide the dough into 6 equal pieces, then roll each piece into 30 inches of rope.
9. Shape each rope into a pretzel, then pinch the ends to lock.
10. Dip the prepared pretzels in soda water and transfer the sheet pan.
11. Bake them for 8 minutes, then brush them with butter.
12. Drizzle salt on top.
13. Serve.

Serving Suggestion: Drizzle sugar and cinnamon on top.

Variation Tip: Add a teaspoon of honey to the dough for a change of taste.

Nutritional Information Per Serving:

Calories 216 | Fat 7.4g |Sodium 435mg | Carbs 24g | Fiber 1.4g | Sugar 1.5g | Protein 7.1g

Cinnamon Rolls

Prep Time: 10 minutes.

Cook Time: 20 minutes.

Serves: 6

Ingredients:

Dough

- 1 cup of milk warm
- ½ cup 1 tbsp granulated sugar
- 1 tbsp Active dry yeast
- 2 large eggs room temperature
- 6 tbsp butter, melted
- 1 tsp pure vanilla extract
- 4 to 4 ½ cups all-purpose flour
- 1 tsp sea salt
- 1 tsp ground cinnamon

Filling:

- 1 cup brown sugar packed
- 2 ½ tbsp ground cinnamon
- 6 tbsp butter, softened

Frosting:

- 1 (8 oz) package cream cheese
- ¼ cup butter softened
- 2 cups powdered sugar
- ½ tsp pure vanilla extract
- 1/8 tsp salt

Preparation:

1. Mix warm milk with yeast and sugar in a mixing bowl.
2. Cover and leave the mixture for 5 minutes.
3. Stir in vanilla, eggs, butter and mix well until sugar is dissolved.
4. Add cinnamon, salt, and flour, then mix in a stand mixer until smooth
5. Knead this dough on a floured surface for 5 minutes until smooth.
6. Transfer the dough to a greased bowl and cover. Leave it for 2 hours.
7. Meanwhile, prepare the filling, mix cinnamon, brown sugar and butter in a small bowl.
8. Roll the prepared cinnamon roll dough on a lightly floured surface into a 24 x12 inches rectangle.
9. Spread the cinnamon filling on top and roll the dough into a log.
10. Slice the log into 12 equal-sized rolls.
11. Place the cinnamon rolls in a 9x13 inches greased baking dish.

12. Cover and leave the rolls for 30 minutes.
13. At 350 degrees F, preheat your oven.
14. Now bake the cinnamon rolls for 20 minutes in the oven.
15. For cream cheese frosting, then blend all the ingredients in a bowl.
16. Pour the frosting over the cinnamon rolls.
17. Serve.

Serving Suggestion: Serve the rolls with a drizzle of chocolate syrup on top.

Variation Tip: Drizzle chocolate chips over the filling to make it chocolaty in taste.

Nutritional Information Per Serving:

Calories 249 | Fat 5.1g |Sodium 262mg | Carbs 43g | Fiber 3.3g | Sugar 18g | Protein 8.9g

Lover's Curry

Prep Time: 15 minutes.
Cook Time: 44 minutes.
Serves: 5

Ingredients:

- 1 (5 lbs.) whole chicken cut up
- 2 limes, cut in half
- 2 cups of coconut milk
- 2 yellow onions, diced
- 2 green onions, diced
- 1 cup yellow raisins
- 4 small potatoes, peeled and diced
- 1 bunch fresh thyme, chopped
- 1 bunch fresh cilantro, chopped
- 6 garlic cloves, chopped
- 3 habanero peppers seeds removed
- 1 1/2 tablespoon yellow curry powder

- 1 tablespoon roasted cumin
- 1/2 tablespoon ground ginger
- 2 tablespoons olive oil

Preparation:

1. Blend habaneros, garlic, green onion, cilantro and thyme in a blender.
2. Add 2-3 tbsp water into the blender and blend again,
3. Rub the seasoning mixture over the chicken, wrap it with a plastic sheet and leave for 30 minutes.
4. Sauté cumin, and curry powder with olive oil in a cooking pot over medium-high heat for 4 minutes.
5. Reduce the heat, then add potatoes and yellow onions, then sauté for 10 minutes.
6. Stir in seasoned chicken, ginger and raisins, then cook for 5 minutes per side.
7. Pour in coconut milk, cover and cook for 30 minutes until the sauce thickens.
8. Adjust seasoning with salt and serve warm.

Serving Suggestion: Enjoy the curry with a dollop of sour cream on top.

Variation Tip: Replace potatoes with carrots for change of taste.

Nutritional Information Per Serving:
Calories 483 | Fat 9.9g |Sodium 207mg | Carbs 15g | Fiber 1.1g | Sugar 11g | Protein 42g

Eggnog Milkshake

Prep Time: 5 minutes.

Cook Time: 0 minute.

Serves: 4

Ingredients:

- 3 cups vanilla ice cream
- 1 cup eggnog
- 1 tsp cinnamon
- 3 gingersnaps crushed
- Whipped cream

Preparation:

1. Blend ice cream, cinnamon and eggnog in a blender until smooth.
2. Pour out and garnish with whipped cream and crushed gingersnaps.
3. Serve.

Serving Suggestion: Serve the milkshake with cinnamon sticks and powder on top.

Variation tip: Add a pinch of nutmeg ground for a change of taste.

Nutritional Information Per Serving:

Calories 182 | Fat 6.3g |Sodium 1021mg | Carbs 31g | Fiber 2.5g | Sugar 1.9g | Protein 12g

Prep Time: 10 minutes.

Cook Time: 0 minutes.

Serves: 12

Ingredients:

- ⅓ cup raw pine nuts
- 2 cups packed fresh basil leaves
- ¼ cup Parmesan cheese, grated
- 1 tablespoon lemon juice
- 2 garlic cloves, chopped
- ½ teaspoon sea salt
- ½ cup olive oil

Preparation:

1. Toast nuts in a dry skillet or 5 minutes, then transfer to a blender.
2. Add basil leaves, parmesan cheese, lemon juice, garlic, sea salt and olive oil.
3. Blend these ingredients together until smooth.
4. Serve.

Serving Suggestion: Brush this pesto to season meat or serve with entrees.

Variation Tip: Add toasted almonds to the pesto for a change of taste.

Nutritional Information Per Serving:

Calories 84 | Fat 6.1g |Sodium 397mg | Carbs 3g | Fiber 3g | Sugar 3.3g | Protein 7.2g

Prep Time: 10 minutes.

Cook Time: 9 minutes.

Serves: 6

Ingredients:

- 2 pounds ripe tomatoes, chopped
- ½ teaspoon salt
- ½ cup white onion, chopped
- ½ cup fresh basil, chopped
- 2 garlic cloves, minced
- 1 French bread
- 5 tablespoons olive oil
- Thick balsamic vinegar
- Maldon flaky sea salt

Preparation:

1. At 450 degrees F, preheat your oven.
2. Layer a baking sheet with parchment paper.
3. Slice the bread into ½ inches thick slices.
4. Place the slices in the baking sheet and brush them with olive oil.
5. Bake the slices for 9 minutes until crispy.
6. Mix tomatoes with salt, onion, basil, and garlic in a bowl.
7. Divide the mixture on top of the baked bread slices.
8. Drizzle balsamic vinegar and salt on top.
9. Serve.

Serving Suggestion: Serve the bruschetta with crispy bacon and eggs.

Variation Tip: Add chopped cucumber to the toppings as well for a change of taste.

Nutritional Information Per Serving:

Calories 146 | Fat 37g |Sodium 1265mg | Carbs 21g | Fiber 6g | Sugar 5.2g | Protein 5g

Christmas Meatloaf

Prep Time: 10 minutes.
Cook Time: 55 minutes.
Serves: 8
Ingredients:

Meatloaf

- 2 eggs
- 1 envelope dry onion soup mix
- ½ c seasoned bread crumbs
- ¼ c chopped dried cranberries
- 1 tsp. parsley
- 1 ½ lb. ground beef

Sauce

- 16 oz. cranberry sauce
- ¾ ketchup
- ½ cup beef broth

- 3 tbsp brown sugar
- 3 tbsp onion, chopped
- 2 tsp cider vinegar

Preparation:

1. Mix ground beef, parsley, cranberries, bread crumbs, eggs, and dry onion soup in a bowl.
2. Spread the mixture in a greased meatloaf pan.
3. Bake the meatloaf for 30-45 minutes in the oven at 350 degrees F, until brown.
4. Prepare the sauce and mix all its ingredients in a pan.
5. Cook the sauce for 5-10 minutes with occasional stirring.
6. Spread the sauce over the baked meatloaf.
7. Slice and serve.

Serving Suggestion: Serve the meatloaf with fresh bean salad.

Variation Tip: Replace cranberries with currants.

Nutritional Information Per Serving:
Calories 419 | Fat 2.5g |Sodium 103mg | Carbs 6g | Fiber 0.5g | Sugar 1.5g | Protein 27g

Berry Parfait

Prep Time: 10 minutes.

Cook Time: 0 minutes.

Serves: 3

Ingredients:

- 3 cups mixed berries
- 1-quart plain yogurt

- 3 cups Granola

Preparation:

1. Divide the Granola into 3 serving cups.

2. Top the Granola with the yogurt and top it with berries.

3. Serve.

Serving Suggestion: Serve the parfait with chopped almonds on top.

Variation Tip: You can also use crushed graham crackers instead of Granola.

Nutritional Information Per Serving:

Calories 396 | Fat 22 |Sodium 167mg | Carbs 7g | Fiber 1.3g | Sugar 1.8g | Protein 14.1g

Brownies

Prep Time: 10 minutes.
Cook Time: 21 minutes.
Serves: 6

Ingredients:

- 10 tablespoons unsalted butter
- 1 1/3 cup white granulated sugar
- 3/4 cup 2 tablespoons cocoa powder
- 1 pinch of salt
- 1 teaspoon vanilla extract
- 2 eggs, cold
- ½ cup all-purpose flour
- 1 cup of chocolate chips

Preparation:

1. At 325 degrees F, preheat your oven.
2. Layer an 8x8 inches baking pan with parchment paper.

3. Mix sugar, butter, salt and cocoa powder in a bowl.
4. Heat this butter mixture in the microwave for 30 seconds.
5. Stir in chocolate chips and heat to melt them.
6. Stir in flour, eggs, and vanilla extract, then mix well.
7. Pour this batter into the baking pan and bake for 20 minutes in the oven at 325 degrees F.
8. Allow the brownies to cool, then slices.
9. Serve.

Serving Suggestion: Serve the brownies with white milk glaze on top.

Variation Tip: Add peppermint and mint chips to the brownies.

Nutritional Information Per Serving:
Calories 258 | Fat 9.7g |Sodium 155mg | Carbs 26.3g | Fiber 1.1g | Sugar 2.2g | Protein 12g

Four-Cheese Mac and Cheese

Prep Time: 5 minutes.

Cook Time: 17 minutes.

Serves: 6

Ingredients:

- 1 (16 oz.) package dried cavatappi
- 3 tablespoons unsalted butter
- ⅓ cup onion, chopped
- 3 tablespoons all-purpose flour
- ½ teaspoon salt
- ¼ teaspoon black pepper
- 2 ½ cups milk
- 8 oz. Gouda cheese, shredded
- 4 oz. sharp cheddar cheese, shredded
- 4 oz. Swiss cheese, shredded
- ½ cup Parmesan cheese, grated
- 1 tablespoon butter, melted

- ½ cup panko
  Cooking spray
- Snipped fresh parsley

Preparation:

1. At medium heat, preheat your broiler.
2. Grease a suitable 3-quart baking dish with cooking spray.
3. Cook pasta in salted water in a cooking pot until soft, then drain.
4. Sauté onion with butter in a saucepan for 3 minutes.
5. Stir in flour, black pepper, salt and milk, then mix until smooth for 2 minutes.
6. Stir in all the cheeses and cook until melted.
7. Toss in boiled pasta and mix well.
8. Mix 1 tsp butter and panko mixture in a bowl.
9. Spread the panko mixture over the pasta.
10. Broil the mac and cheese for 2 minutes.
11. Garnish with parsley.
12. Serve warm.

Serving Suggestion: Serve the mac and cheese with crumbled bacon on top.

Variation Tip: You can make this meal by adding shredded chicken or diced ham as well.

Nutritional Information Per Serving:

Calories 397 | Fat 22g | Sodium 121mg | Carbs 30g | Fiber 3.3g | Sugar 7.5g | Protein 21g

Dorito Casserole

Prep Time: 10 minutes.
Cook Time: 58 minutes.
Serves: 8
Ingredients:

- 2 teaspoons olive oil
- 1-pound ground beef

- ½ cup onion, diced
- 1 packet taco seasoning
- 1 ½ cups salsa
- 1 cup sour cream
- 2 cups cheddar cheese, shredded
- 4 cups Dorito chips
- 1/2 cup tomatoes, diced
- 1/4 cup green onions, sliced
- Cooking spray
- Sour cream, cilantro and taco toppings

Preparation:

1. At 375 degrees F, preheat your oven.
2. Grease a 2-3-quart baking dish with cooking spray.
3. Sauté beef with olive oil in a large pan over medium-high heat for 5 minutes until brown.
4. Stir in onion and sauté for 4 minutes.
5. Add red salsa, and taco seasoning, then cook for 4 minutes.
6. Remove the pan from the heat and add sour cream.
7. Mix well and keep this filling aside.
8. Crush the Doritos and spread 1/3 of the chips in the prepared dish.
9. Top the chips with ½ meat filling, and then add 1/3 Doritos and 1/3 cheese.
10. Repeat the chips, meat and cheese layers.
11. Add chips and cheese on top, then cover with a foil sheet.
12. Bake the casserole for 30 minutes in the oven.
13. Uncover and bake the casserole for 15 minutes in the oven.
14. Garnish with green onion, sour cream, taco seasonings, olives and tomatoes.
15. Serve warm.

Serving Suggestion: Serve the casserole with mayo or yogurt sauce.

Variation Tip: If you don't have Doritos, use crushed tortilla chips to make this casserole.

Nutritional Information Per Serving:
Calories 420 | Fat 11g |Sodium 341mg | Carbs 25g | Fiber 12g | Sugar 1.7g | Protein 22.3g

Buttercream

Prep Time: 10 minutes.
Cook Time: 0 minutes.
Serves: 6

Ingredients:

- 5 oz. butter softened
- 10 oz. icing sugar

2 tbsp milk

¼ tsp vanilla extract

Preparation:

1. Beat butter in a mixing bowl until soft.
2. Stir in sugar and beat until fluffy.
3. Stir in milk and vanilla extract.
4. Mix well and serve.

Serving Suggestion: Enjoy this buttercream on top of cupcakes.

Variation Tip: Add orange extract and orange juice for change of taste.

Nutritional Information Per Serving:

Calories 104 | Fat 7.5g |Sodium 143mg | Carbs 16g | Fiber 3.5g | Sugar 1.9g | Protein 11g

Prep Time: 5 minutes.
Cook Time: 0 minutes.
Serves: 4

Ingredients:

- 1 cup of orange juice
- 1 cup of pineapple juice
- ¼ cup lime juice
- ¼ cup rum
- ¼ cup dark rum
- ½ cup of grenadine

Preparation:

1. Mix rum, grenadine, dark rum, lime juice, pineapple juice and orange juice in a pitcher.
2. Garnish with ice, orange slice and maraschino cherries.
3. Serve.

Serving Suggestion: Serve the punch with a bowl of fresh fruits.

Variation Tip: Add watermelon juice for change of taste.

Nutritional Information Per Serving:
Calories 130 | Fat 0g |Sodium 136mg | Carbs 31g | Fiber 4g | Sugar 63g | Protein 2g

Guacamole

Prep Time: 10 minutes.

Cook Time: 0 minutes.

Serves: 8

Ingredients:

- 3 avocados, peeled, pitted, and mashed
- 1 lime, juiced
- 1 teaspoon salt
- ½ cup onion, diced
- 3 tablespoons fresh cilantro, chopped
- 2 Roma (plum) tomatoes, diced
- 1 teaspoon garlic, minced
- 1 pinch ground cayenne pepper

Preparation:

1. Mash avocados in a bowl, then add tomatoes, garlic, cilantro, onion, salt, lime juice and cayenne pepper.
2. Mix well, cover and refrigerate for 1 hour.
3. Serve.

Serving Suggestion: Serve the guacamole with nachos.

Variation Tip: You can also add chopped jalapeno for a change of taste.

Nutritional Information Per Serving:

Calories 131 | Fat 15g |Sodium 157mg | Carbs 19g | Fiber 0.2g | Sugar 21g | Protein 5g

Bourbon Barbecue Sauce

Prep Time: 5 minutes.
Cook Time: 10 minutes.
Serves: 6
Ingredients:

- 1 cup ketchup
- 1/2 cup bourbon
- 3 tablespoons brown sugar
- 3 tablespoons mild molasses
- 3 tablespoons apple cider vinegar
- 2 tablespoons Worcestershire sauce
- 1 tablespoon soy sauce
- 1 tablespoon Dijon mustard
- 11/2 teaspoons liquid smoke
- 1 teaspoon onion powder
- 1 teaspoon garlic powder
- 1/2 teaspoon dried crushed red pepper
- 1/2 teaspoon black pepper

Preparations:

1. Mix ketchup, bourbon, brown sugar, molasses, apple cider vinegar, Worcestershire sauce, soy sauce, and the rest of the ingredients in a saucepan.
2. Mix and cook for 10 minutes with occasional stirring.
3. Serve.

Serving Suggestion: Brush the sauce meat and poultry for BBQ.

Variation Tip: Add honey instead of molasses for change of taste.

Nutritional Information Per Serving:
Calories 83 | Fat 1.7g |Sodium 110mg | Carbs 37g | Fiber 1.4g | Sugar 6.5g | Protein 1.6g

Cheeseburger Sliders

Prep Time: 10 minutes.
Cook Time: 40 minutes.
Serves: 6
Ingredients:

- 2 lbs. ground beef
- 1 teaspoon salt

- 2 teaspoons pepper
- 2 teaspoons garlic powder
- ½ white onion, diced
- 6 cheddar cheese, slices
- 12 dinner rolls, cut in half
- 2 tablespoons butter, melted
- 1 tablespoon sesame seeds

Preparation:

1. At 350 degrees F, preheat your oven.
2. Mix beef with garlic powder, black pepper and salt in a greased 9x13 inches baking dish.
3. Spread the beef evenly, and bake for 20 minutes in the oven.
4. Cut the rolls in half, lengthwise and place the bottom halves in another baking dish.
5. Spread the cooked beef on top of the rolls.
6. Drizzle onion and cheese on top.
7. Place the remaining rolls on top and brush them with butter.
8. Drizzle sesame seeds on top and bake for 20 minutes in the oven.
9. Slice and serve warm.

Serving Suggestion: Serve the sliders with creamy coleslaw.

Variation Tip: Add crispy bacon to the sliders as well.

Nutritional Information Per Serving:

Calories 356 | Fat 21.2g |Sodium 121mg | Carbs 25g | Fiber 0.9g | Sugar 5g | Protein 26g

Prep Time: 10 minutes.

Cook Time: 10 minutes.

Serves: 6

Ingredients:

- 16 oz mozzarella cheese block
- 2 large eggs
- 2/3 cup Italian style breadcrumbs
- Salt, to taste
- Black pepper, to taste

Preparation:

1. Cut the cheese block into ½ inch sticks.
2. Beat eggs with black pepper and salt in a bowl.
3. Spread the breadcrumbs on a plate.
4. Dip the cheese sticks in the egg mixture, then coat them with the breadcrumbs.
5. Place the sticks in a tray, cover and refrigerate for 2 hours.
6. At 365 degrees F, preheat your Air Fryer.
7. Spread the mozzarella sticks in the air fryer basket.
8. Air fry the mozzarella sticks in the air fryer for 5-10 minutes until golden brown.
9. Toss the sticks once cooked halfway through.
10. Serve warm.

Serving Suggestion: Serve the sticks with tomato sauce.

Variation Tip: Use crushed cornflakes for the coating for a crispy texture.

Nutritional Information Per Serving:

Calories 341 | Fat 37g |Sodium 982mg | Carbs 14g | Fiber 0.2g | Sugar 3.5g | Protein 23g

Three Bean Salad

Prep Time: 10 minutes.

Cook Time: 0 minutes.

Serves: 6

Ingredients:

For the salad

- ½ red onion, chopped
- 2 celery stalks, chopped
- 1 (15-oz.) can garbanzo beans, drained
- 1 cup loosely packed, fresh, chopped
- 1 (15-oz.) can kidney beans, rinsed and drained
- 1 teaspoon fresh rosemary, chopped
- 1 (15-oz.) can cannellini beans, rinsed and drained

Dressing:

- 1/3 cup apple cider vinegar
- ¼ cup granulated sugar

3 tablespoons olive oil

- 1 ½ teaspoons salt

¼ teaspoon black pepper

Preparation:

1. Mix all the beans, celery, onion, rosemary, parsley in a salad bowl.
2. Add all the apple cider dressing ingredients to a bowl, then mix well.
3. Pour this dressing over the bean salad, then mix well.
4. Serve.

Serving Suggestion: Serve the salad with sautéed greens.

Variation Tip: Add sautéed green beans to the salad as well.

Nutritional Information Per Serving:

Calories 265 | Fat 7.9g |Sodium 1114mg | Carbs 32g | Fiber 0.3g | Sugar 5g | Protein 17.2g

Hollandaise Sauce

Prep Time: 10 minutes. Cook Time: 5 minutes. Serves: 12

Ingredients:

- 4 egg yolks
- 1 tablespoon lemon juice
- 1/2 cup unsalted butter, melted
- Pinch cayenne
- Pinch salt

Preparation:

1. Beat egg yolks with lemon juice in a stainless-steel bowl until the mixture is thick and fluffy.
2. Place this bowl in a pot filled with boiling water and stir in butter.
3. Cook and mix the egg yolks until thick and pale in color.
4. Remove the sauce from the heat and add salt and cayenne.
5. Mix well and allow the sauce to cool.
6. Serve.

Serving Suggestion: Enjoy this sauce with poached eggs and bread.

Variation Tip: Sprinkle a pinch of white pepper for a change of taste.

Nutritional Information Per Serving:

Calories 99 | Fat 22.8g |Sodium 780mg | Carbs 11g | Fiber 7.5g | Sugar 9.7g | Protein 1g

White Wine Spritzer

Prep Time: 5 minutes.
Cook Time: 0 minutes.
Serves: 2

Ingredients:

- 3/4 glass white wine
- 1/4 glass club soda
- Slice of lime

Preparation:

1. Mix white wine with club soda in a pitcher.
2. Serve with a lime slice on top.
3. Enjoy.

Serving Suggestion: Serve the drink with lemon twists.

Variation Tip: You can add fresh lemon juice for a refreshing taste.

Nutritional Information Per Serving:

Calories 103 | Fat 0g |Sodium 393mg | Carbs 15.8g | Fiber 3.5g | Sugar 2g | Protein 2g

Butternut Squash Soup

Prep Time: 10 minutes.
Cook Time: 30 minutes.
Serves: 4

Ingredients:

- 2 cups vegetable stock
- 4 garlic cloves, peeled and minced
- 1 carrot, peeled and chopped
- 1 Granny Smith apple, cored and chopped
- 1 onion, peeled and chopped
- 1 sprig of fresh sage
- 1 butternut squash, peeled, seeded and diced
- 1/2 teaspoon salt
- 1/4 teaspoon black pepper
- 1/8 teaspoon cayenne
- 1 pinch ground cinnamon
- 1 pinch nutmeg

- 1/2 cup canned (unsweetened) coconut milk
- Coconut milk, smoked paprika, optional

Preparation:

1. Add butternut squash, stock, garlic, sage, onion and the rest of the ingredients to a cooking pot.
2. Cook the squash soup for 30 minutes on a simmer.
3. Puree the cooked squash with a hand blender until smooth.
4. Serve warm.

Serving Suggestion: Serve this soup with a dollop of sour cream on top.

Variation Tip: Add some boiled potatoes to the soup for more taste.

Nutritional Information Per Serving:

Calories 342 | Fat 20g |Sodium 63mg | Carbs 33.5g | Fiber 1g | Sugar 11.3g | Protein 26g

Chicken and Waffles

Prep Time: 15 minutes.
Cook Time: 30 minutes.
Serves: 6

Ingredients:

Chicken:

- 1 cup buttermilk
- 1 ½ pounds chicken pieces
- 1 1/4 cups flour
- 1 teaspoon smoked paprika
- 1/8 teaspoon cayenne pepper
- 1/2 teaspoon salt
- 1/2 cup cornmeal
- 1/4 teaspoon black pepper
- Peanut oil for frying

Waffles:

- 1 cup yellow cornmeal
- 1 cup all-purpose flour
- 2 teaspoons baking powder
- 1/2 teaspoon baking soda
- 1/4 teaspoon salt
- 2 cups buttermilk well shaken
- 2 eggs
- 1/4 cup maple syrup
- 4 tablespoons butter melted
- 1 cup cheddar cheese shredded
- 1 bunch scallions sliced
- 1 tablespoons chive, minced

Preparation:

1. Mix flour with black pepper, salt, cornmeal, smoked paprika and cayenne pepper in a bowl.
2. Add buttermilk to a bowl and dip the chicken in the buttermilk.
3. Coat the chicken with the flour mixture and shake off the excess.
4. Add oil to a deep cooking pan and heat it to 350 degrees F.
5. Deep fry the chicken in the cooking oil until brown.
6. Transfer the prepared chicken to a plate lined with a paper towel.
7. Mix flour with baking soda, baking powder, salt and cornmeal in a bowl.
8. Stir in buttermilk, maple syrup, butter, an egg, then mix well until smooth.
9. Add cheese, scallions, and chives, then mix well.
10. Set up the waffle iron and preheat it.
11. Add a scoop of the batter to the waffle iron and cook for 5-7 minutes.
12. Cook more waffles in the same manner.
13. Serve the chicken with the waffles.

Serving Suggestion: Serve the chicken and waffles with hot sauce.

Variation tip: Add a pinch of lemon zest to the chicken coating for a change of taste.

Nutritional Information Per Serving:
Calories 468 | Fat 24g |Sodium 715mg | Carbs 54.3g | Fiber 4g | Sugar 16g | Protein 28g

Prep Time: 10 minutes.

Cook Time: 25 minutes.

Serves: 6

Ingredients:

- 2 ½ cups flour
- 3 tsp baking powder
- 1 tsp salt
- 1 ½ cups sugar
- 1/2 cup shortening
- 2 eggs
- 1 cup milk
- 1 tsp vanilla

Preparation:

1. Mix 2 ½ cups flour, baking powder, salt, and sugar in a bowl.
2. Beat shortening with milk in a bowl at low speed for 2 minutes.
3. Stir in vanilla and eggs, then beat for 1 minute.
4. Add flour mixture and mix until smooth.
5. Divide this batter into two 9-inch greased baking pans.
6. Bake the batter for 25 minutes at 375 degrees F in the oven.
7. Allow the cake to cool.
8. Serve.

Serving Suggestion: Serve the cake with cream cheese frosting on top.

Variation Tip: Sprinkle a drizzle of cinnamon sugar powder on top.

Nutritional Information Per Serving:

Calories 348 | Fat 12.2g |Sodium 421mg | Carbs 41.1g | Fiber 3.3g | Sugar 14g | Protein 11g

Sloppy Joe Sandwiches

Prep Time: 10 minutes.
Cook Time: 50 minutes.
Serves: 2
Ingredients:

- ½ pound ground beef
- ½ onion, chopped
- ½ cup ketchup

- 2 tablespoons water
- 1 tablespoon brown sugar
- 1 teaspoon Worcestershire sauce
- 1 teaspoon prepared mustard
- 1 teaspoon white vinegar
- 1 teaspoon chilli powder
- ¼ teaspoon garlic powder
- ¼ teaspoon onion powder
- ¼ teaspoon salt
- 2 hamburger buns, split

Preparation:

1. Sauté onion and beef with oil in a skillet for 10 minutes until brown.
2. Add salt, garlic powder, onion powder, vinegar, mustard, chilli powder, Worcestershire sauce, brown sugar, water and ketchup.
3. Mix well, cover and cook the beef for 40 minutes on low heat until soft.
4. Serve warm in the buns.

Serving Suggestion: Serve the burgers with mayo sauce.

Variation Tip: Add some chopped bell pepper for a change of taste.

Nutritional Information Per Serving:

Calories 421 | Fat 17g |Sodium 585mg | Carbs 32.5g | Fiber 0.4g | Sugar 1.8g | Protein 26g

Personal Pizza

Prep Time: 10 minutes.
Cook Time: 25 minutes.
Serves: 6

Ingredients:

- 2 (6-1/2 oz.) packages pizza dough
- 1 ½ cups pizza sauce
- 1-pound ground beef, cooked
- 1 medium onion, chopped
- 1 cup green pepper, chopped
- 2 cans (2-1/4 oz.) ripe olives, sliced

- 2 cups mozzarella cheese, shredded

Preparation:

1. Divide the prepared pizza dough into 6 portions and spread each portion into an 8-inch circle.
2. Place these circles in two baking sheets and bake them for 10 minutes at 425 degrees F.
3. Divide the beef, onion, green pepper, olives and cheese on top of the crusts.
4. Bake again for 15 minutes in the oven.
5. Serve warm.

Serving Suggestion: Serve the pizza with tomato ketchup.

Variation Tip: Add sliced jalapenos on top for change of taste.

Nutritional Information Per Serving:
Calories 445 | Fat 26.3g |Sodium 393mg | Carbs 37g | Fiber 0g | Sugar 1g | Protein 24g

David's Big Cookies

Prep Time: 10 minutes.
Cook Time: 10 minutes.
Serves: 8
Ingredients:

- 4 ½ cups crispy rice cereal
- 1 ¾ cups all-purpose flour
- 1 teaspoon baking soda

- ½ teaspoon salt
- 1 cup butter, softened
- ¾ cup white sugar
- ¾ cup light brown sugar
- 2 eggs
- 1 teaspoon vanilla extract
- 2 cups chocolate chips

Preparation:

1. At 350 degrees F, preheat your oven.
2. Grind rice cereal in a food processor into a fine powder.
3. Mix 1 cup cereal powder with salt, baking soda, and flour in a bowl.
4. Beat butter with brown sugar and white sugar in a bowl.
5. Stir in eggs and vanilla, then mix well.
6. Add cereal mixture and whisk until smooth, then fold in chocolate chips.
7. Divide the batter into spoonful cookie rounds on a greased cookie sheet.
8. Bake the cookies for 10 minutes in the preheated oven.
9. Allow the cookies to cool for 10 minutes.
10. Serve.

Serving Suggestion: Serve the cookies with warm milk or hot chocolate.

Variation Tip: Add cacao nib to the cookie dough.

Nutritional Information Per Serving:

Calories 231 | Fat 17g |Sodium 123mg | Carbs 32.6g | Fiber 0g | Sugar 20.5g | Protein 5g

Prep Time: 10 minutes.

Cook Time: 0 minutes.

Serves: 8

Ingredients:

Bottom Layer

- ½ cup unsalted butter, diced
- ¼ cup granulated sugar
- 5 tbsp unsweetened cocoa powder
- 1/8 tsp salt
- 1 egg, beaten
- 1 ¾ cup graham cracker crumbs
- ½ cup almonds, chopped
- 1 cup sweetened shredded coconut

Filling:

- ½ cup unsalted butter softened
- 3 tbsp heavy cream
- 2 tbsp custard powder
- 1 ¾ cups powdered sugar

Top Layer:

- 4 oz semi-sweet chocolate, chopped
- 2 tbsp unsalted butter

Preparation:

1. Grease an 8x8 inch baking dish and layer it with parchment paper.
2. Melt butter in a bowl, then add salt, cocoa powder, and sugar, then mix well.
3. Stir in beaten egg and return the mixture to a double boiler.
4. Cook until the mixture thickens, then remove it from the heat.
5. Stir in almonds, coconut and crumbs.
6. Mix well and spread the mixture in the baking dish.
7. For the filling, blend all its ingredients in a bowl with a hand blender.
8. Spread this filling in the crust.
9. Melt chocolate and butter in a bowl for the top layer by heating in the microwave.
10. Pour the chocolate melt on top of the filling.
11. Allow the layers to set, cover and refrigerate for 1 hour.
12. Slice and serve.

Serving Suggestion: Serve the bars with white chocolate melt on top. **Variation Tip:** Add chopped pine nuts to the filling.

Nutritional Information Per Serving:

Calories 112 | Fat 7.8g |Sodium 171mg | Carbs 41g | Fiber 3.4 | Sugar 18.2g | Protein 2g

Fruit Cups

Prep Time: 10 minutes.

Cook Time: 0 minutes.

Serves: 18

Ingredients:

- 1 can (12 oz.) pineapple juice concentrate
- 1 can (6 oz.) orange juice concentrate

- 1 cup of water
- 1 cup of sugar
- 2 tablespoons lemon juice
- 3 medium bananas, sliced
- 1 package (16 oz.) frozen unsweetened strawberries
- 1 can (15 oz.) mandarin oranges, drained
- 1 can (8 oz.) crushed pineapple
- 18 clear plastic cups

Preparation:

1. Mix pineapple juice concentrates with orange juice, water, sugar, lemon juice, bananas, strawberries, oranges, and pineapple in a bowl.
2. Divide the mixture into plastic cups and freeze for 50 minutes.
3. Serve.

Serving Suggestion: Serve the cups with strawberry skewers on top.

Variation Tip: Add crushed strawberries and raspberries to the cups.

Nutritional Information Per Serving:
Calories 115 | Fat 0g |Sodium 52mg | Carbs 30g | Fiber 2g | Sugar 32g | Protein 1.2g

Harvest Smoothie

Prep Time: 5 minutes.
Cook Time: 0 minutes.

Serves: 2

Ingredients:

- 2 beets, peeled and diced
- 2 celery stalks, diced
- 2 apples, peeled and diced
- 1 ½ cup plain yogurt
- 1 cup almond milk
- 2 tbsp agave

Preparation:

1. Blend beets, celery stalks, apples, yogurt, milk and agave in a blender until smooth.
2. Serve.

Serving Suggestion: Serve with mint leaves on top.

Variation Tip: Add avocado flesh to the smoothie.

Nutritional Information Per Serving:

Calories 192 | Fat 2g |Sodium 350mg | Carbs 32g | Fiber 3g | Sugar 10g | Protein 5.8g

Sex in a Pan

Prep Time: 10 minutes.
Cook Time: 20 minutes.
Serves: 6
Ingredients:

Crust

- 1 cup pecans chopped
- 3 tbsp granulated sugar

- ½ cup unsalted butter melted
- 1 cup all-purpose flour

Cream cheese layer

- 8 oz cream cheese
- 1 cup powdered sugar

- 1 cup cool whip

Vanilla pudding

- 5 oz instant vanilla pudding

- 2 cups of milk

Chocolate Pudding

- 5 oz instant chocolate pudding

- 2 cups of milk

Toppings

- 2 cups cool whip

- shaved chocolate

Preparation:

1. At 350 degrees F, preheat your oven.
2. Grease a 9x13 inches baking pan with cooking spray.
3. Blend all the crust ingredients in a blender and spread the mixture in the prepared baking pan.
4. Press the crust and bake for 20 minutes in the oven.
5. Meanwhile, prepare the vanilla pudding and mix instant vanilla pudding with milk in a saucepan.
6. Cook this vanilla pudding on low heat until it thickens, with occasional stirring.
7. Prepare the chocolate pudding and mix instant chocolate pudding with milk in a saucepan.
8. Cook this chocolate pudding on low heat until it thickens, with occasional stirring.
9. Allow both the puddings to cool at room temperature.
10. Beat cream cheese with sugar and cool whip in a bowl until fluffy.
11. Spread the cream cheese mixture over the baked crust.
12. Top this layer with vanilla pudding, then add chocolate pudding on top.
13. Garnish with whipped cream and chocolate.
14. Cover and refrigerate for 4 hours.
15. Slice and serve.

Serving Suggestion: Drizzle cocoa powder or chocolate sprinkles on top.

Variation Tip: You can add a caramel layer to add more taste.

Nutritional Information Per Serving:

Calories 171 | Fat 19g |Sodium 157mg | Carbs 31.4g | Fiber 1.7g | Sugar 8.5g | Protein 2.9g

Crunchy Peanut Butter Thins

Prep Time: 10 minutes.
Cook Time: 30 minutes.
Serves: 8

Ingredients:

- 1/2 cup all-purpose flour
- 1/2 cup whole wheat flour
- 1/4 cup rolled oats
- 1 tablespoon wheat germ
- 2 teaspoons chia seeds
- 1/2 teaspoon salt
- 1/4 teaspoon ground cinnamon
- 1/3 cup peanut butter
- 1/3 cup brown sugar
- 3 tablespoons vegetable oil
- 1 large egg white
- Cooking Spray
- 1 oz. bittersweet chocolate, melted

Preparation:

1. At 350 degrees F, preheat your oven.
2. Layer a 9x13 inches baking pan with aluminium foil and grease with cooking spray.
3. Mix flour, cinnamon, salt, chia seeds, wheat germ and oats in a bowl.
4. Beat egg white with vegetable oil, brown sugar and peanut butter in a bowl for 2 minutes.
5. Stir in flour mixture and mix until smooth.
6. Spread the dough in the prepared pan and bake for 30 minutes in the oven.
7. Drizzle melted chocolate on top and allow it to set.
8. Cut the thins into squares.
9. Serve.

Serving Suggestion: Serve the peanut butter thins with chocolate syrup.

Variation Tip: Add crushed nuts to the peanut butter thins.

Nutritional Information Per Serving:

Calories 112 | Fat 12g |Sodium 167mg | Carbs 44.3g | Fiber 2.4g | Sugar 17g | Protein 1.6g

Latte

Prep Time: 10 minutes.
Cook Time: 10 minutes.
Serves: 2
Ingredients:

- 2 cups of milk
- 1 ⅓ cups hot brewed coffee

Preparation:

1. Add milk to a saucepan and cook over medium-low heat until foamy.

2. Pour the hot brewed coffee into 4 serving cups.
3. Add warm milk on top, keeping its foam back.
4. Divide the foam on top of the latte.
5. Serve.

Serving Suggestion: Drizzle coffee or cocoa powder on top.

Variation Tip: Add some whipped cream to the warm milk.

Nutritional Information Per Serving:

Calories 162 | Fat 12.1g |Sodium 41mg | Carbs 20g | Fiber 0g | Sugar 8g | Protein 1.8g

Prep Time: 5 minutes.
Cook Time: 0 minutes.
Serves: 1

Ingredients:

- 3 oz. gin
- 3 oz. fresh lemon juice
- 1 tablespoon granulated sugar
- 1 1/2 cups ice cubes
- 1 cup chilled Champagne
- Lemon twists for garnish

Preparation:

1. Mix gin, ice cubes, sugar, and lemon juice in a cocktail shaker.
2. Pour into the serving glass and pour the Champagne on top.
3. Garnish with a lemon twist.
4. Serve.

Serving Suggestion: Serve the champagne toast with lemon zest on top.

Variation Tip: Add olives to the glass before pouring out the drink.

Nutritional Information Per Serving:

Calories 143 | Fat 0g |Sodium 74mg | Carbs 32.4g | Fiber 2.6g | Sugar 16.2g | Protein 0.2g

Conclusion

Did you like those Schitt Creek recipes? Don't they take you back to the amazing and captivating life of the famous hamlet of Elmdale County? Well, if you are reading this part of the book, then you must have already picked up your most favorite Schitt Creek meals out of our collection. And if you are still wondering to select the best one out, then there is no better way than to try the different recipes from this book and taste and test to find the one you like the most.

In a nutshell, the content of this book brings you one step closer to that small town of Elmdale in a way you might have never explored before. The aim behind creating these simple and amazing recipes was to bring the same Motel Rosebud life to your home. So, let your creativity shine in the kitchen and make the world taste the fineness of your cooking techniques. There are a number of recipes that were inspired by the whole series. Some of the popular recipes from this collection are:

- Sloppy Jocelyn's
- There's a Dead Guy in Room 4-Cheese Macaroni
- Twyla's Meadow Harvest Smoothie
- Farm Witches' Peanut Butter Things
- Rosebud Motel Cinnamon Rolls
- Budd's Bourbon BBQ Sauce

The entire length of this book discusses similar recipes and many others that are inspired by all the special moments of the television series. It's about time that you cook some and enjoy your Schitt Creek inspired meals anywhere and anytime. These recipes are also an amazing way to impress all the Schitt Creek's fans in your circle. Let's get started!

www.ingramcontent.com/pod-product-compliance
Lightning Source LLC
Chambersburg PA
CBHW082125240725
30131CB00005B/29